PowerUP!

Find and use your potential, talents and dreams!
Understand how to remove limiting thought patterns
so you can go from dream to reality!

MERETHE DRØNNEN-SCHMIDT

Norlights Publishing

ISBN-13: 978-82-999353-1-9

DEDICATION

This book is dedicated to all those who have been hindered from becoming the best versions of themselves, by having wrong thought patterns. Let me have the pleasure of motivating you to discover and put off limiting thoughts that might have hindered you to achieve your potential, and assist you in the process of recovering your lost dreams!

CONTENTS:

PREFACE

The goal of this book that you now have in front of you is to help you in your process of renewing yourself by giving you renewed power and strength to achieve your goals.

There are a lot of books on the market that encourage the readers to think positive, but they do not give you any understanding of what to do if you fall back into old destructive thought patterns. To be able to unlearn destructive thought patterns, it is essential to understand how thought patterns are being established in the human mind. One must take the right steps at the right places in the process. Just by wishing a positive change in your life will not lead you there. Only a real change of thought patterns, which again will influence your behavior, is the way to go to establish a permanent change in your life. Many are fighting destructive thoughts about themselves, about who they are, how far they can go and what they can do. Positive thinking alone will not remove these. Others have stopped dreaming, and many wish to be a better version of themselves, to reach their full potential.

In this book you will learn cognitive techniques that will help you remove limiting thoughts from your mind, so that you can think powerful thoughts about yourself and your opportunitites. Additionally it will give you a concrete tool so that you can start taking new steps in your life.

The life you live is your life,- and no matter what you have experienced earlier in life, you can decide today to take some steps to reach new goals in your own life!

POWER-UP!

POWER-UP!

1. DO YOU SEE YOUR POTENTIAL?

All people are born with a great God-given potential, gifts, talents and dreams. Do you use your potential and do you see your possibilities for growth?

Are you living your full potential and do you use your opportunities?

Do you have a dream about becoming, doing or working with something else than you do today? Or- have you met limitations in your life that have made you stop dreaming?

Have you put your dream on the shelf? Or have you

1

stopped dreaming? Have you given away the control over your own life and future to "voices" that are negative, pessimistic and destructive on your behalf?

Are you surrounded by positive people or by people that tear you down, take away your dream and make you less than you are?

There are many things that can influence us throughout life with both positive and negative events leaving their marks. Sometimes repeated negative influences from our closest surroundings will do something to us. We can stop to dream and loose faith in ourselves.

No matter what our surroundings are like, we must decide to never give up hope. Neither must we give away the leadership of our own lives. We are the ones that should sit by the rudder of our own boat in the ocean of life.

Did you know that what you think about yourself and your possibilities, have a crucial influence for you in your life?

We are all born with dreams, hopes and special

unique abilities and gifts to reach our potential. Though sometimes it is our own thoughts that are limiting our lives. I believe that the dream you carry inside of you has the power to lift you out of the thought pattern that says you will never achieve your dreams.

Did you know that you are unique and that there is only one copy of you? Do you know that who you think you are, what you think you can do- actually decide how far you will reach in life?

Think about the fact that there is not one human being on this earth that has the same fingerprints that you have! Exactly your finger print is unique! You are in fact quite special,- and you are created to be so. Look around you. Don't you see a variety of different personalities, gifts and talents?

We are all unique and we are all diverse. Different in diversity. No two of us are alike. Even identical twins do not have the same fingerprints.

Have you ever reflected over how and in which way

we humans are made so differently? Think about how many different interests and professions that exists. We need plumbers, electricians, medical doctors, farmers, teachers and a lot of others professions. We are all created different, and not two of us are alike... Why do some love intricate details while others love to focus on "the big picture"? If Einstein and Newton did not love to go in depth about physics and chemistry, what would the world look like then?

Some of us have an outlook on life at a macro level, while others have a preference for the details at a micro level. Some prefer a perspective of breadth, others at depth. For some it is natural to look at the world and humans from a scientific or realistic view and for others it is more natural to see the world from a relational or psychological view. No worldview is better than the other, and collectively we are all supplementing each other. A whole society of individuals with different life callings, goals and directions.

But what happened with all the unique human beings

that were born on this earth?

Why have so many died as copies and only meer shadows of who they could have been? Have you ever thought that you have a greater potential than what you have realized in your life until now? If yes, what do you think is necessary to exploit and use more of your potential that lies latent inside of you?

These are important questions to reflect about, and only you are the one that can answer these questions and fulfill your life. You are the one that have the key for your life, and only you can decide to search for the "gold" inside of you, to overcome limitations and start using your potential. It is possible! But, as with all work with change, it demands a conscious effort from you.

No matter what has happened to you in your life, whatever the impact has had on you,- today is the first day of the rest of your life. You decide what to do with it.

POWER-UP!

6

2. YOUR POTENTIAL, TALENTS AND DREAMS

How can one unveil and find one's potential?

The first step is to gain consciousness about the fact that we are all born with godgiven gifts and talents. Everyone is good at something! All of us are also born unique, as originals, even though many dies as copies.

We are and shall be different, different and unique - in diversity.

What is the dream in your heart? What is your passion? What do you dream about doing or being?

It is important to search for the dream in one's inner self to carry out one's full potential. We have all heard or read about people in a retirement home that say; "if I only had dared to do this or that". If I only had taken the chance and done something about those thoughts and dreams I had. "You see, I dreamt about travelling and living in another country for a year when I was younger,- but I didn't".. or; "I dreamt about dancing ballet"... or "I had a dream about taking acting classes, but I didn't have enough courage"... "I always dreamt about learning to fly a plane" might someone say. "If I could have lived my life again, I would have dared to take the chance".

To accomplish something, one must also take the chance to fail. Way too many play it safe and do not dare to take a step out of the comfort zone to take some new steps,- to get something new in their lives. The ordinary and customary wins over daring to take the chance to step out into the unknown. This is the second important step.

Ben Saunders was a chubby and shy boy that never was selected to play at any sport-teams. He was ridiculed and laughed at by his classmates. When Ben was 15 years old, he got a bike as a gift, and started to bike together with a jogging friend. Gradually he became in better shape, and one day he made a decision to build his body by strength and endurance training. When he was 18, he ran his first marathon. Later, and based on a meeting with a man who had become famous for rowing an open boat over the Atlantic ocean, a new dream started inside of Saunder. This time about becoming a polar explorer. Saunders started goal-oriented ski training and later became the youngest person to ski the North Pole alone. Later, he also became the first person to ski roundtrip from the Antarktis to the South Pole.

Twyla Tharp was a woman from Indiana that carried a big dream inside about becoming a dancer. She went to New York City to study and had a large desire to carry out her big dream. Everywhere she went on audition for dance roles, she heard that she did not have the technical abilities to become a ballerina. She was also told she was too short. She started to doubt if she ever would become a professional dancer. One day she decided to start her own dance-ensemble and make her own dancing style. This group practiced persistently every day in the basement of a church in Greenwich Village. The few jobs they got, paid them little, and they hardly received any recognition.

40 years later, Tharp had choreographed more than 100 dance performances on Broadway and in famous movies like Hair and Ragtime. She even won the National medal of the Arts in 2004! Why? Because she never gave up her dream, and worked hard towards reaching her goal.

In my own life, it were those times when I took the chance to step into the unknown that gave me the most joy and satisfaction. To have won over one's own -and other's- limiting thoughts, is a great joy and satisfaction.

When I was 26 and a single mom, I carried inside a dream to further my education. I wanted to study psychology and eventually do work within the human resource field. I heard from a for me "significant person" in my surroundings that I should be content with working as an cleaning assistant at my mother's hairdressing-saloon,- while many others pointed out that I was way too old to start studying. Many people said that I could not be a single mom and study as well, because it was too demanding .

Today, 20 years later, I have 10,5 years of higher academic education behind me, I am in my third and final year of my Ph.D.-studies and have worked eight years as a personnel manager. If I had believed in those voices that said that I could not juggle parenthood and furthering my education, I have never been where I am today!

I could have chosen to listen to the well-meant advice, and lived a more simple and different life today. Instead, I would have been dissatisfied and had less self-confidence, because I would not have maximized my true life potential. This ultimately would have caused a certain type of dissatisfaction in my life going forward.

If I had wanted to, I could have had many reasons against moving to Oslo and start studying psychology. Reasons like I got a no both to kindergarten and to a family apartment, or that I didn't know anybody in this town etcetera.

An example of what I did, was also something that both Twyla and Saunders and any many others have done, I forced my thoughts to dwell on the opportunities, the positive and the solutions- and not just on the limitations and the negative aspects.

To refuse to let what one sees and hears steal one's dream. Don't let go of them, and treasure your dreams like gold!

But of course, -it is also necessary to take steps that are in accordance with the dreams. Because:

Faith without action is a dead faith.

Letter of James

It is not enough just to sit around and think positive. One must of course also take the necessary steps of actions towards reaching the goals.

To receive something new one must also do something new! This is a slogan I made up in my youth, and has always been a motto in my life since then.

I have a dream!

Said Martin Luther King. He stood in 1963 in front of 250 000 Afro-Americans at the memorial of Abraham Lincoln in Washington DC, and told them about their dream of a state and a nation without oppression and racism. These were new words, put forward with courage and a strong vision for the future, in an époque of time where strong racism and suppression against black people were common.

This speech based on Martin Luther King's dream and vision for America made a difference for the black American politics. If he didn't hold fast to his dream and taken brave steps towards challenging other Afro-Americans and white people to follow his new vision, then parts of American society might have looked much differently today.

Oprah Winfrey said that:

"The biggest adventure that you can have is to live your life from your dreams".

She has also lived in the conviction that she was *"destined for greatness".* This is something we all should do. We are all destined to reach our greatest potential, and I dare to contend that your thoughts about how far you can go, are actually limiting you in exactly how far you will go.

A well-known American basketballstar Michael Jordan, stated that he used to visualize that he would be the greatest basketballplayer in the history. He let that be the ruling words in his life.

Henry Thoreau said that *"our truest life is when we are awake in our dreams"* and
Oscar Wilde wrote; *"Ordinary riches can be stolen, real riches can not. In your soul lies infinite precious things that can not be stolen from you".*

Do you have a dream? What is your dream?

Everything starts with a dream, a thought, an idea. You should protect your dreams like they are gold. Don't tell your dream to those you know will suppress you and take your dream away from you. Even if they might not have bad intentions, -and it is simply their need for everyday predictability that drives them,- it is of the uttermost importance for you to dare to take the first step!

I believe that we all have dreams we carry deep inside. I also believe that the godgiven dream inside of you has the power to lift you out of the thought that says that you will never fulfill your dreams.

I believe:

"You are never given a dream without the opportunity to fulfill it".

Then the question is; What is your dream?

Someone might have let the monotony of everyday

life take over and have simply stopped dreaming. But the dream is there! Just search and you will find them. Maybe your dream is furthering your education. Start a shop? Write a book? Take a flight certificate? It is never too late! Maybe you are dreaming about carrying out a new hobby, but have not yet taken any steps towards realization? No matter how big or small your dream is,- it is just as important. It is *your* dream, and *you can* carry it out.

Here are some questions that will help you in searching for your dream. Sit down and quietly look at one question at a time. Listen to your inner voice and discover the thoughts that comes to your mind. Look back and let the thoughts come up to the surface. Find the thoughts that give you joy to think about.

- Is there something that you have a clear dream about doing or being, but have put away?

- What do you believe is your heart's deepest wish?

- What are the thoughts, visions or dreams that you can't get out of your mind?

- Where is your passion?

- In what area do you produce good results?

- What feels natural for you to do?

- What type of tasks do you feel joy about doing?

- What kind of profession do you wish you had?

- What gives you happiness to think about?

- If there were no limitations in your life, what would your life look like?

- If there were no limitations of time, education or money, where would you live, and what would be your profession?

- When are you fully engaged? What are your
  favorite subjects?

To carry out one's potential, it is important to clarify
one's dream. Take a pen and paper and write down your
answers on paper which will make them more clear.
These answers will be followed up later in the book.

Some think that they do not have dreams, but that is
wrong. Everyone have a dream and something they
dream about being or doing deep inside. One just has to
search it out.

In my earlier work as a pedagogical-psychological
advisor I met many young people that did not believe in
themselves or the future. Some were "given up upon" by
their teachers and/or parents. Their scholarly
achievements were low, and they could exhibit bad
behavior and make noise in the classroom. The teachers
had given up on them, and needed help to get the pupils
on the right track.

The only key that could open up the locked façade in the youth, was when he or she opened up the door to their heart and started to talk about what they liked and what they dreamt about. At that point, even the toughest youth could open up, and a little piece of joy and enthusiasm would come to the surface. Before reverting back again. This was a process, and things take time. Nevertheless, this is a key that can open up human hearts and it is such moments one sees that a dream lives in every human person. Everyone has a dream! Everyone is good at something! We have different strengths and weaknesses, and in a society we all fit in and complement each other! Just look, go exploring your inner self, and behind many layers of self-defense you will find your dream.

But- if your thoughts are more filled with fear, limitations and lack of belief in yourself- you must challenge yourself to reveal and discover if there are any destructive and negative thought patterns you carry with you.

Only then can you replace them with a new set of

thoughts. This is what this book is about. To help *you* take new steps in your life. That is a joy for me.

Let's now first take the round to discover which thoughts you are thinking about yourself today. There is a big chance that you will find limiting thoughts that you don't really want to have, -and that you would like to receive some assistance in removing. If you, like the most of us, have thoughts that put limits on how far you have programmed yourself to go; thoughts that have put you in a box "for those that do not dare" or "those that do not manage", it is about time to take a grip on those wrong thought patterns and get rid of them.

To get you started so that you can begin to map out your earlier forces of influence, it is necessary to take a trip to your past to search for possible causal factors. Things that have made you think limiting thoughts about yourself, reasons to why you might have given away your dream, or lost confidence in yourself and your possibilities.

POWER-UP!

3. YOUR THOUGHTS TODAY

"What a man sows, he will harvest" is an old saying from the Proverbs. To sow can involve much, but in this particular setting, it involves thoughts, attitudes and actions. A farmer knows that to harvest, he must first sow. He can not just sit around and think about sowing, -he must actually do it. Everything starts with a seed. In a way your thoughts are seeds. A thought is always the first step towards an action. It is important to plant good seeds in one's own mind by sowing good and constructive thoughts. We must "water" our thoughts with nutrition, which means positivity and thoughts about succeeding. We need to think plus-thoughts and not minus- thoughts. Plus-thought fills us with energy and hope, minus-thoughts drag energy out of us and fills us with dissatisfaction and hopelessness. We must take control over our thoughts and fill our minds with positive thoughts.

Those thoughts that earlier in your life were sown into your heart's soil, are what you are harvesting today. We actually do choose our future, based on what we sow into our thougths today. Thoughts about who we are and what our strengths are, what we can do and what we can achieve in life. Only when we become aware of our thought patterns can we become free from the negative and reinforce the positive. We can in fact decide to do this.

Research has shown that solution-focused counseling has a more positive effect in a shorter time than what problem-focused counseling do. (Stams, Dekovic, Bust and DeVries, 2006). The same results have been found in areas of a) leadership and coaching (Caufffman, 2007) b) mental health treatment (de Shazer, 1985, 1994; Bannink, 2005) and d) in work with disabled children (Westra and Bannink, 2006).

To set one's mind to focus on solutions rather than

weaknesses, have a bigger influence on the human mind and thoughts than one could believe.

You will be surprised over how many people that do not know their strengths, and have not even thought about them".
Fred Riddick, Psychologist.

Do you know your strengths?

Are you aware of which thoughts you are thinking daily and do you understand which thoughts are working in your mind when you meet challenges? It is relatively important to recognize one's own thought patterns. Only in this way you can get rid of the negative thoughts.

Did you know that research has discovered that between 50 to 75 % of the effect of anti-depressive medication represents the placebo-effect? (Kirsh et al, 2008; Leuchter et al, 2002). That means that the expectations to feel well by taking the pills, actually influences one to feel well after taking them. Research therefore showed that in 50 to 75 % of the cases where humans were told they received real medication against depression, they became well even if they took a placebo pill.

The placebo effect can just as well be used for your own advantage.

Humans with negative thought patterns can with a bit of practice be changed to have a more optimistic view on their possibilities and options in life (Green, 2008). Do you choose to self take control over your thoughts and expectations?

Research has also shown the existence of a strong link between self-efficacy (belief in one's own abilities to achieve) and psychological health (Bauer & Bonnanno, 2001; Bandura, 1977). Bauer and Bonnanno found in a study that the language pattern used in our evaluations of ourselves, have a longtime effect on our psychological health. What you believe about yourself affects many parts of your life, in addition to influencing your future.

What you expect and believe you can do, can even, according to the researchers, influence your weight! The researchers Weinberg, Hughes, Critelli, England and Jackson (1984) studied the faith in one's own ability to achieve weight loss, and found that those that had a high degree of belief in one's own ability to loose weight, lost more weight on those 8 weeks the study lasted, than those who did not have such high belief in own ability. Additionally, the researchers found that the location of control (inner or outer) the person believed he/she had, predicted the size of the weight loss! Those who were inner control driven, that means those who believed that the control over the circumstances were controlled by inner forces in themselves, tended to loose more weight than those who had an outer control focus (those whose faith in one's own decisions and life were controlled by factors outside themselves, which they cannot influence).

Researchers at NTNU in Norway found that out of normal weight teenagers that felt fat during adolescence, 78 % of them became overweight as adults. That was a significantly higher degree than what the youths that did not feel fat during adolescence scored (NTNU, 2012).

Paus, Petrides, Evans and Meyer (1993) found in a study that just by *thinking* about a behavior, actually activated the same area of the brain (in anterior cingualated cortex (ACC)) that is activated by *doing* that behavior (Rosenthal & Jacobsen, 1977). That means that if you think a sad thought, your body will recognize the sadness and thereby react in the same way as if you experienced something sad. If you think about something positive, your body will react as if something positive actually happened to you. We know that when we are happy, our bodies produce "happiness-hormones" (endorphines) that stream around in our bodies. For a moment, imagine love that you have experienced. Imagine how happy you were, and how it appeared in your physical body. How it was feeling like jelly in your knees, and the heartbeat you had when you saw the person you were in love with. Depending on your age, you might get a smile on your face now or maybe even laugh a bit of yourself. The memories create joy just by thinking about them. Endorphines, which are hormones of joy, are released in your body.

Isn't this exciting? It means that if you decisively lead

your thoughts into positive paths, when you have a tendency to do the opposite, your body will in the outer consequence change the production of hormones and actually set free hormones of joy or sorrow in your body.

If we go to a completely different field; the leadership field, research has shown that out of all types of leaders, those leaders that had higher belief in their own abilities to achieve, more often showed important leadership abilities and leader behavior than those with lower levels. Additionally, those leaders with higher belief in themselves, also showed larger effectivity at work than those with lower levels of belief in their own ability to achieve (Chemers, Watson & May, 2000).

This tells us something about the breadth of areas in life where your attitude of what you can *do*, *be* or *manage*, is influencing your actual behavior.

Most of us do not have insight and clarity into all our thoughts and how we think in different situations. In this book I will take you on a travel in your own mind, where you can get some assistance in the process of discovering and making your dreams and goals more clear. An important part of this travel will be to search for wrong thought patterns, understand the reasons to why you might have them, in addition to get some strategies to replace them with plus-thoughts. This is important for breaking off the limitations in your thought and mind, and replace lack of confidence and belief in yourself and your possibilities with positive solution-oriented thoughts. Which again will lay the foundation for your behavior and expectations.

POWER-UP!

4. WHICH FACTORS HAVE INFLUENCED YOU?

Do you know which factors in your childhood, adolescence and culture that have influenced your attitudes, thoughts and patterns of behavior? -Your attitude towards yourself? -What you can do and how far you can go?

A wise philosopher once said that a human is not free before he/she knows what has been shaping and influencing him/her, and what has shaped his/her attitudes and opinions.

Do you know if you have adopted the public opinion of X and Y, or if you front your own beliefs? Do you dare to stand alone against the public opinion? Do you stand up for yourself? Despite other's opinions?

Wrong thought patterns can keep us imprisoned in

defeat! Maybe someone influential for you has spoken negative words in your life. Maybe someone told you that you are never going to succeed, that you will never reach your goals, -because you don't have what it takes to get there.

Don't listen to these lies!

Instead, break out of the limitations from the past and let your thoughts dwell around new, positive can-do attitudes! Breaking these barriers will change your life!

No matter what you have experienced in the past, no matter how many defeats you have experienced or who or what has hindered your progression, -today is a new day with new opportunities!

Don't let your past decide your future.

An illustration of this is a done study done among prisoners in Texas which showed that 85 % of all the prisoners in that study that had a parent or close relative that had been jailed at one time in life. Attitudes and "accepted behavior" is actually something that can be inheritable; a set of inherited attitudes that has been passed along the generations from a family, a group, a country or a culture. Prisoners can birth new prisoners...

But this is not something one just must "inherit". Attitudes can be created. To be aware of one's own thought patterns, can lead to one being able to see patterns that needs to be broken. So they can be replaced by new and more constructive thought patterns.

This is something one can consciously work on and make decisions to say "no, I don't want to have that pattern in my life". I want another future. This is about a) being conscious of one's own thought patterns, good as well as bad, and b) decide to work with how one thinks, break the pattern of negative thought power that make the foundations for the actions we choose to take. One can decide to create a new standard. No matter what the challenge is.

Poverty? Alcoholism? Depression? Anger? Low self esteem? —one can choose to set a new standard. Don't declare yourself to be not able to create a new standard in your life by saying this is impossible. In this way you limit yourself and your possibilities to create a new life.

What has influenced you?

What has shaped your attitudes?

How has your self confidence been shaped?

Influence from different environments

What makes a person become as he/she becomes, and what is it that really has power to influence a person's thoughts and attitudes?

Humans are being influenced from different sources and cultures around us. Bronfenbrenner (1995, 1998) divided these areas into micro-, ekso-, meso- and macro-levels.

The *Micro-level* are immediate environments we are directly involved in, like family, neighborhood, classes we have been/ are parts of, scouts, gymnastics etc.

Influences from the *Ekso-level* are formal and informal societal constellations that we are not directly involved in.

The *Macro-level* are the superstructure of formal and informal institutions at the society level, like a country's laws and regulations, values and customs etc.

We all belong to different environments at the same time. Nobody belongs to only one environment. We get urges from all the environments, and bring the urges with us into other environments.

The micro- and the meso- levels are concrete manifestations of the higher macro system. For instance the school policy and school ideology. Another example is the politics that include the distributions of a country's economic assets. This again influences lower levels of environment like for instance a family's economy, welfare, free school, the amount of kindergartens and other economical distributions in a society.

The Meso-level is the level above the micro-level and refers to the relationships between the different microsystems and the coherence between the different contexts. For instance the relations between family experiences and school experiences, the groups of neighbours and the groups of friends.

One experience in a micro-level environment will

possibly influence another. For instance will a child that has been rejected by his/her parents, possibly carry with him/her a feeling of rejection towards other grown-ups in other micro-levels, for instance at school.

The Ekso-level is the third level and speaks about how for instance a parent's working hours indirectly can influence a family situation at home. A parent who for instance travels much, will have much absence from home, which again can influence the child's childhood and adolescence at different levels. For instance may the interaction between the child and the parent that is not home, be different than if the parent spent more time at home.

Another example, taken from the debate in Norway, is the option of regulating work hours to six-hour working days. If this would be regulated from the government, it would necessarily influence and characterize children and families in a different way than what a ten-hour-workday would. We know that different countries, as well as different organizations, have different working hours, and this influences the families' situations at home.

In this we see that both the country and the part of the world we are born in, as well as the particular family and the particular local environments we have grown up in, have influenced our attitudes and opinions strongly. Some are we aware of, others we are not. The school system in a country have many explicit societal functions, seen or hidden, that are actualized through the school's concrete policy. The schools have for instance the job to front mutual values, norms and policies that are representative for a country's politics. Teachers we have met every day during school-time have shaped us and influenced us to become the persons we have become. Our parents and our closest family we have grown up together with, have had the strongest influential force over us, and parental opinions and attitudes have inevitably invisible been "transferred" to become ours without being aware of it.

It is therefore of uttermost importance to reflect over what are our own real values and attitudes, and what are derived from other sources. Maybe you are a woman that grew up in a country that does not permit that women should work or maybe an unwritten rule exists in your family that women should not have an education. Such norms and rules are influencing us strongly, and even if a woman growing up in such a culture should move to another country, this view will continue to influence how men look at women and women look at themselves, if they do not confront these issues. But they must want to do it.

In this way we have inherited a lot of both invisible and visible thought patterns from family, school, friends, community and country,- which have shaped us to become the people we have become. Those thought patterns that I want you to go looking for and reflect over, are those thoughts that you unconscious (or even conscious) have received as your own- and that are limiting you in your efforts to reach your goals in life.

If you have what I call a "poverty"-mentality and identity,- you might even go around with a lot of limiting thoughts about what you can achieve in for instance your economy. You might already have put yourself into a box (probably something similar to those that your parents had) where you have "programmed yourself" to a) first take an education b) thereafter work a few years and save some money before you buy an apartment. Then you c) buy a little house before you d) buy a bigger house and e) thereafter have paid down your loans before you f) sell the house and buy a smaller flat and give inheritance to your children. This is the way most of us think.

But why not buy a bedsit while you are studying? In this way you get into a narrow property market, and the installments you pay on your loan, are actually savings and investment that you will actually keep. If the house market prices in addition are increasing, you will also end up possibly making some extra money while you have "lived for free" those years. Why not buy an apartment with a bedsit, where the bedsit income are paying off large amounts of your loan?

Why choose a long education, if a shorter one can allow you to reach the same goal? You don't need to think in a box, and you don't need to buy a little house without rent income,- if a slightly bigger house can give you rent income that covers a large part of your loan. Bigger rent incomes gives as known bigger loan possibilities in the bank.

Liberate yourself from limiting thought patterns and explore various different ways of doing things. A Norwegian saying states;" there are many ways to Rome". You don't need to walk down the main street. You can select another road, if this way is a shorter way to achieve your goals.

Another important factor that is influencing what you can accomplish, is how you look at yourself and your expectations. This is the theme of the next chapter.

POWER-UP!

POWER-UP!

5. VIEW OF SELF AND EXPECTATIONS

Then how is our own apprehension of who we are and what we can do?

Our view of self is mainly shaped by two factors;

- Other people's expectation of you
- Your own expectations

Other people's expectations of us have a strong influence on our behavior. On the other side, we also have our own expectations. We expect that if we behave in a certain way, certain things are going to happen. These expectations are based on experience and learning.

If our experiences are to be transferred into expectations, it is of the utmost importance how we interpret and understand these experiences.

Additionally will our self view contribute to shape our expectations. Herein lies a deep secret according to the strong motivational power the view of self gives.

Other people's expectations of you

Studies have shown that other people's expectations of us are influencing our view of self. A well-known example is the study by Rosenthal and Jacobsen about the "Pygmalion in the classroom". This classroom experience showed that when a teacher was told that the pupils in one particular class performed at lower levels than pupils in other classes, the teacher would lower his level of teaching and expectations of these pupils. Soon, these pupils started to perform at a lower level, no matter their level of intelligence or abilities (Rosenthal & Jacobsen, 1968).

And opposite, when teachers were told that a certain class of pupils (actually it was the same class of pupils mentioned above!) performed at higher levels, the teachers went into that classroom with a total different attitude and started to teach at a higher level. The teacher expected more of each pupil. These pupils' view of themselves were actually influenced by what the teacher expected of them. This is how it is with all of us. We have a tendency to set the expectations of our performance at a level that is in accordance with what other people in our surroundings are expecting of us. This is something I numerous times have experienced in classrooms where I have been observing, in my job as a pedagogical- psychological advisor. So, we are definitely influenced by other people's expectations of us,- as well as our self-expextations.

The same happens in our surroundings. That could be at the working place or in the family. A person that has grown up in a family where he/she has been picked on or continuously heard that he/she does not match up, will carry with him/her this expectation further in life, if he/she do not become aware of and break these destructive thought patterns. And opposite, if a person mutual times have heard that he/she is competent and capable, this will be an established thought pattern after a while.

A well-known psychologist and sociologist George H. Mead made a theory that is known as "symbolic interactionism". This theory explains how our view of self is shaped, in interaction with how (for us) significant and important others view us. These "significant and important others" can for instance be our parents, our spouse, our boss or our teacher. For the other person's assessment of me to be of importance for my view of self, it must be a person that means something to me in one way or another.

How these "important others" affect us and our behavior is experienced and interpreted by us individually, therefore influencing our self-esteem. In this way we are shaping our self-worth based on what other people think about us. We are reflecting other people's reaction about us in a mirror. Our identity and view of self is shaped by taking a step outside of oneself, and taking other peoples' perspective through social relations (Martin & Gillespie, 2010; Walker, 2010).

Our own expectations

Only what you have seen in your thoughts, can be birthed.

Rene Decartes

This saying emphasizes the importance of holding on to the expectations. It is important to understand that not a single outer influence can have a mark on us and steer our behavior without going through ourselves and our own filter of personal interpretations and explanations.

An important part of this process is what makes the foundation for our own *expectations*. How we evaluate and interpret the different situations around us will be of importance for which expextations we will have for what will happen next.

That means that when our experiences are transferred to expectations, our interpretations and understanding of these experiences have conclusive influence.

In the process of interpreting and understanding our experiences, everything that happens with and around us will be observed and filtered and put into our own personal world, where the things we are experiencing are given meaning.

Two people can experience the same, but have two different interpretations. Depending on how the experience is being understood and filtered, which again is based on earlier experiences. Next, the individual will add value and meaning to this interpretation. Some can interpret the same type of experience as success based on own inner strength, while others can interpret this as mere coincidences. More about this in the next chapter.

POWER-UP!

POWER-UP!

6. INTERPRETATION OF SUCCESS AND FAILURE

Now that you know how your own and other people's expectations to us are influencing our view of ourselves, I'll present another important process. Namely, our inner process of examining and adding meaning and causality to an occurrence. Thereafter I will illuminate some facts about the differences between women and men in this area.

Do you interpret the reasons for your success due to inner or outer causes?

Do you know your own pattern of thoughts, and do you know if you have a tendency to attribute your *successes* to inner or outer causes? Do you know if you are interpreting your failures to inner or outer causes; - within or outside yourself?

This is of importance for you to know about. Because it is first when you have uncovered which thoughts that have been established within you, that you can take action and change your thoughts with new patterns.

Weiner was one who researched humans' attributions to success and failures (Weiner, 1979, 1986, 1992, 1995, 2000; Weiner, Graham & Reyna, 1997; Weiner & Kukla, 1970).

Humans have different ways of interpreting reasons to success and failures. Different people have different habits of interpreting. Weiner (1977, 2000) used the categories location, stability and controllability to explain why people interpret and attribute reasons to success and failure differently (Weiner. 1977, 2000).

Location tells something about whether the occurrence is attributed to sources within the person him/herself (inner causes) or to sources outside the person (outer sources). If the explanation is given to inner factors, this person will look at him/herself as the originator to, and as the one responsible for the occurrence. If on the other hand, the explanation is given to outer sources, it is called outer attribution. An example of an outer attribution is to explain the incident as luck/bad luck, blaming the boss, neighbor or for instance the particular assignment, as the reason for why something went good or bad.

If you are one who often uses an inner causal attribution explanation on your achievements, you will most often describe your own contributions as hard work or to your good or bad abilities.

The factor *stability* will tell something about the attributions' stability over time. Unstable causes are reasons that are variable. Were you for instance tired or ready for work? Did you exert a low or a high effort?

Was the reason why the result became so good because of help from others or simply by luck?

Controllability in an attribution explains something about whether you feel that you have control over the causes of the reasons why it went good or bad. A controllable reason to you performing good, can for instance be the level of difficulty, or your abilities. A controllable reason could for instance be the factor that you are working frequently and well, because you make an all-out effort and so on. You experience to be in control over the causes.

All these factors are of conclusive meaning for which expectations you are establishing. The way you explain the incident to yourself will actually decide your expectations for succeeding or not succeeding;- and if you look at yourself as one who have the leading role in your own life or not. Do you feel that you have control over the incident,- or do you feel that you don't? If you are a person that often explains for instance positive incidents as luck and coincidences, the positive incident will not be anchored according to your own production. The same goes for people that often have statements like "I am not good enough" or "the assignments are too difficult for me".

If you think about it for a moment and ponder how this will effect your expectations for the result of your own efforts, you will most surely say that this way of interpreting the causes of the incident, will give a feeling of the control being outside yourself. You simply expect that coincidences and incidents outside yourself are deciding the outcome.

As you probably now understand, there is a great coherence between your causal attribution and your expectations of the results of your own contributions. If you are a person that says about yourself that you do not have influence on diverse incidents and that the cause of the incidents lie outside of your control, you can quickly come into a situation where you feel powerless. "Nothing works" and "I can't do anything about this". In the psychological language it is called "learned helplessness" and tells about a state of being where a person feels without power and without influence over his/her own situation. The attribution lies in uncontrollable inner factors; "I am not good enough" and "nothing of what I do will change the situation". This results in an attitude that says that "no matter what I do, no matter how much I give,- it won't work because I am not good enough". Or outerly explained; "these circumstances make it impossible for me to succeed".

Will this attitude produce expectations for

succeeding?

Expectations that says it is possible to make an effort yourself?

Expectations for being an initiator who can implement things in one's own life?

Or will this lead to a negative spiral where lack of results (because of lack of effort!) will result in expectations of failure?

Do you see how dangerous this way of thinking is? It is a real poison for creativity, initiative and the outlook of oneself as an actor with self-determination in one's own life.

It is incredibly important to look at oneself as a person who can start, cause and control incidents in one's own life! If a person gives himself over to helplessness, the person will no longer feel in charge of his own life,- and that is a dangerous place to be. No matter the reasons for being in this condition, it is never too late to work oneself out of it!

It demands a conscious deprogramming of your inner

thought patterns, and that is something that is possible! You can actually choose to steer your own thoughts. You can choose which thoughts you want to dwell on, and you can choose which thoughts you want to say "no thanks!" to. The most important part is to find the thoughts you are already lead by.

Think back to the example with the "pygmalion in the classroom". Just like the teacher was told that the pupils in that particular class were good, they became even better! If you decide to show yourself as much love that you will help yourself change an old negative thought pattern,- then you are kind to yourself! Will you give yourself that opportunity? If having helped other people with this- you also owe it to give yourself this help you need to get on a better track of becoming a better version of yourself! You deserve that! Decide today to give yourself a chance.

For something new to appear in your life
you have to do something new!

-But it demands a greater effort from you. Are you willing to try?

Do you know that research has shown that the feeling of helplessness is a main ingredient in depression? Also, the feeling of not having control, is one of the main ingredients in learned helplessness. BUT,- and this is important!,- this is under the control of emotional, motivational and cognitive processes! (Pryce, Azzinnari, Spinei, Seifritz, Tegethof and Meinlschmidt, 2011).

That means that YOU by taking control over your thoughts (part of the cognitive processes) also can steer yourself out of learned helplessness. You can motivate yourself, and thereby take the actor place and not the passive seat in your own life. You do not need to let your emotions, or your feelings at the moment, rule over you. You can decide to "throw away" thoughts that give you negative feelings.

Imagine for a moment that you have achieved your goals. Visualize how it looks, and that you are being met by others in a positive way. Feel how you straighten up your back, and sense the good feeling of mastery, and what it feels like.

How does it feel? Really good?

Do you want that feeling to be a more frequent feeling in your own life?

But maybe you are one of those who are not able to see that you can reach your goals. Maybe you have given yourself over to mediocrety according to reaching your real potential. It could be that you are having difficulties looking further than day to day, and maybe you need assistance in changing your thought patterns. Baumeister (2012) found that prolonged experiences with control-deprivation; that means the lack of control over a certain period, leads to an attitude closer to "learned helplessness". When you instruct yourself that incidents and circumstances are outside of your control (sources not inside of you),- you will think thoughts that will contribute to feelings of "learned helplessness".

Research have also shown that counseling and help to understand and handle the situation, can actually un-learn the state of "learned helplessness"! (Gottschall &

Stefanou, 2011). And this is good news!

YOU can NOW decide to take the lead in your own life and future!

Martin Seligman, a well-known psychologist, did a study among depressed persons. The depressed persons received the assignment of writing down three positive happenings every day, instead of focusing on the state of, and the reason to, their depression. Part two of this research involved the depressed people forming groups where they encouraged each other to notice and focus on the positive happenings that occured during the day. As much as 94 % of the participants' depression decreased significantly! From clinically strong symptoms of depression to clinically mild and moderate symptoms of depression. The effect was like the effect of medication and cognitive therapy combined! (Rob & Schwartz, 2007).

This is really good news! By turning the focus from the negative to the positive,- the level of depression and hopelessness decreased. This is something I of all my heart wish that you will receive into your own life, no matter what level of challenges that you might have. You can really take some grips and change your life to the better by your willingness to work with your own thoughts!

Do you want more examples? Here is an example from the school sector and how successful and unsuccessful students are reasoning in their inner thinking.

Lebedina-Manzoni (2004) found in her study that successful students (those who received good grades) estimated the reason for their success due to inner factors (personal characteristics) such as perseverance, good ability to organize, the ability to acquire knowledge etc. Namely to an inner, stable ability or characteristic. Those students that did not have such success, meant that many of the reasons to succeed at school lied in sources outside themselves; in the environment and surroundings outside of their control. Parents, type of exam, whether the content was interesting etc. (Lebedina-Manzoni, 2004). Lebedina-Manzoni pointed out that a treatment of the students without success should be based on cognitive restructuring of negative thoughts. In turn this helps to think more positive thoughts.

Differences between women and men

A lot of research have shown that there are marked differences between men and women according to causal attributions of success and failure (Bar-Tal & Frieze, 1976, 1977; Guest, Peeccei & Rosenthal, 1996; Deux, 1979). Women have a tendency to interpret and explain the sources of their successes according to unstable, outer factors. For instance luck and easy assignments, while men more often interpret their successes to inner, stable factors.

Looking at the interpretation of failure, we see the opposite picture; women are quicker to interpret and explain their failures as lack of ability, then what men do. Women have lower expectations of themselves and their performances.

Guest, Peccei & Rosenthal (1996) posited that type of attribution could be a reason to differences between male and female leaders. Since leadership jobs often demand a type of self-promoting behavior according to career progression as a leader, this could give women certain challenges. Female leaders can attribute their own actions in such a way that it limits the feel of feeling competent. Additionally, the causal attribution will possibly influence on which type of expectations to achieve a person has (Guest, Peccei & Rosenthal. 1996).

Deaux (1979) found in a research that female leaders causally attributed less often their successes to the factor ability than what men did. The same results did Guest (1996)find in his research (Guest, 1996).

If we compare Weiner's (1977) classification of causal attributions in the last chapter, to male and female patterns, we find something interesting.

We will then see that **women** more often than men causally attribute:

-**their successes** to **outer** factors (others, the environment), and then most likely unstable factors like luck/ not luck or help from others,

-while **men** more often causally attribute their **successes** to **inner**, stable causes like for instance abilities or good work.

Bold = Men. <u>Underlined</u>= Female.

	Inner Attribution (one self)		Outer Attribution (other, environment)	
	Stable	Unst-able	Stable	Unstable
Un-cont-roll-able	**Ability**	Tired, mood	Difficulty in assigment	<u>Luck/ not luck</u>
Con-troll-able	**Good work**	All-out-effort	Teacher, boss, assignment	<u>Help from others</u>

Table 1. From Weiner (1979, p.7): Interpretation of the sources to success, classified after cause, stability and controllability. Here: also added female and male differences according to causal attribution pattern.

When it comes to interpretations of failure, we see the following differences between male and females illustrated:

<u>Underlined</u>= Female. **Bold** = Male.

	Inner Attribution (oneself)		Outer Attribution (others, environment)	
	Stab-le	Unst-able	Stable	Un-stable
Un-cont-roll-able	<u>Abil-ity</u>	Tired moo d	Assign-ment difficulty	**Luck / no luck**
Cont roll-able	God work	All-out-effort	Teacher, the boss the assign-ment	Help from others

Table 2. From Weiner (1979, p.7): Interpretations of failure, classified after cause, stability and controllability. Here: also added differences between male and female according to attribution pattern.

It is here seen that women tend to causal attribute their failures to inner causes (within themselves) like for instance abilities, while men tend to attribute their failures to outer unstable causes like luck/ not luck.

Aren't these differences of utmost importance or what?!

The same type of results are found between people with low and high self-esteem. That means that persons with high self-esteem have the same type of causal attributions as men /boys in general have.

These differences can be cultural influenced and show the "culturally right thing to do" according to sex roles in a socialization process, but can also be based in other causes. These research results show a tendency between the sexes, and of course one can also find both attribution categories in both the sexes.

Anyway,- the most important thing is- that you *can* start working with your own thoughts today, if your own thought patterns are weakening you. You can reprogram your existing thoughts with help of cognitive techniques for change of behavior. That means that you, by understanding the existence of this, can choose to start reprogramming and thinking differently, based on a choice you take. Isn't this exciting?

Even if this is not a book about sex differences, it is important to point out that since women have a tendency to explain success to outer factors (luck) and interpret failure to inner causes (lack of ability), it is important to work with the attitudes and beliefs in one's own abilities in women and girls.

Many studies have also shown that men and women that perform at the same level, give different causal attributions of their own behavior (Bar-Tal & Frieze, 1976, 1977; Nichols, 1975; Wiegers & Frieze, 1977). These studies showed that women had a tendency to interpret the reasons to their own behaviors less favorably than what men did. They attributed more seldom their own successes to their own abilities, and had a tendency to believe that their weak results were based in lack of abilities. Good results were more often than men, explained by outer factors such as luck etc. Men tended to explain their own good results with inner stable abilities.

This is something I have seen numerous times in my job as a personnel manager. Men bragged more often of their own abilities than females did. I often heard women degrade themselves and their abilities in interviews, while I observed that men more often did the opposite. This was an interesting thing to observe, and confirmed to me that these differences actually exist.

This pattern of explanation can also influence women and their expectations of themselves and their own attitude in the work place, as well as in other life arenas. If you are a woman and can recognize these thoughts within yourself, I will encourage you to work on these thought patterns. If you are a man and you recognize these thought patterns as your own, I will of course also encourage you to take some grips. I wish with all my heart that people should start seeing their own potential, and break down destructive thought patterns that keeps them imprisoned in defeat.

You CAN become a better version of yourself!

How you causal attribute your own behavior and how you view your possibilities, are connected to your motivation to perform. More about this in the next chapter.

7. HOW THE ATTRIBUTION MODEL IS CONNECTED TO THE MOTIVATION TO PERFORM

How you attribute your successes and failures are connected to the motivation you have to achieve. In other words; how you interpret your successes or failures, is connected to which motivation you have/will have to further perform. I find that extremely interesting. That means that if you interpret a positive incident/ success to be connected with your inner factors,- you will have more motivation to perform! We all want to perform better and more,- so this is really an area where you can decide to focus your attention on, as to acquire a new positive change in your life.

The motivation to achieve is therefore connected to

the expectations to succeed, and in one's own beliefs and abilities. If you are one that tends to point out your own abilities when you explain why you succeed, you most likely have a high motivation to achieve.

And remember what was mentioned in a previous chapter about how expectations are creating new expectations through our inner evaluations and interpretations. Isn't it about time to decide to work with yourself to change your pattern of attribution for the better?

Summed up, one can say that the process that occurs inside of us goes through these stages:

1) We are born into and are grown up in a particular environment that are influenced by the various macro-, ekso-, meso- or micro-levels that were mentioned in chapter 4.

2) This makes the foundation for your expectations. Which are built on a) your belief about yourself and b) others' expectations to you.

3) This is what you bring with you when you act and interact in different settings in life.

4) You explain your actions according to your

existing scheme/ your existing patterns of thoughts.

5) This again shapes the foundation for your new expectations/ attitudes towards different occasions in life.

6) Thereafter the circle continues back to step 2, which again lays the foundation for step 3, 4, 5 etcetera.

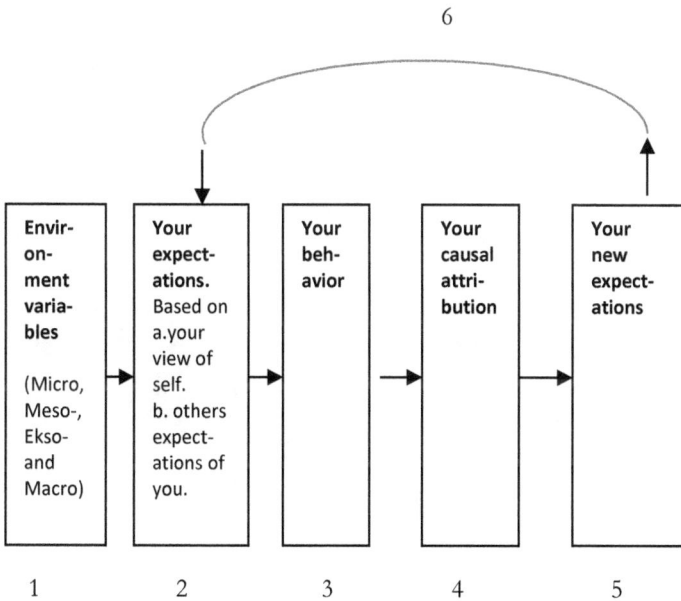

6

Envir-onment variables (Micro, Meso-, Ekso- and Macro)	Your expect-ations. Based on a.your view of self. b. others expect-ations of you.	Your beh-avior	Your causal attri-bution	Your new expect-ations

1   2   3   4   5

Figure 1. Frame of interpretation and patterns of action.

This is your frame of interpretation and your patterns of action. If you are going to change one set of patterns which have lasted throughout your life,- you must go through this circle. The positive thing is that you can yourself choose to change your frames of interpretation, and thereby establish a new foundation for new expectations and actions. More about this in the next chapter.

POWER-UP!

POWER-UP!

8. CAN OUR ATTRIBUTIONS BE CHANGED?

The answer is definitively YES! Based on what you have read in the previous chapters, you have received confirmation that patterns of interpretation can be changed!

But it is essential that you see the coherence between your own behavior and the consequences it reaps. The most important thing is to see oneself as the source of,- and thereby as responsible for an action. You must see yourself as the one in charge of your own life,- and not as a piece that is moved around by others.

You can therefore actually do something concrete to strengthen your inner motivation. By working at your patterns of interpretation, you can motivate yourself to achieve your own goals and plans for the future.

That means that you:

- Can be aware of the thought patterns that keep you down

and:

- Replace them with thoughts that bring growth in your life!

"As a person thinks, so is he"
Proverbs

What do you think about yourself?

What you think about yourself is an extremely strong influental factor in your life.

Who you think you are, what you believe you can do, what you believe you can be, what you believe about your life and your possibilities;- have a stronger influence over you than the politics or our society or economy will ever have!

You cannot live in continuous self-pity, and then wonder why your situation doesn't change!

- Think small, believe small and expect small. And then they wonder why big things never happen to them. It's their own thoughts that keeps them down.

Do you set your standards too low?

- Imprison and get rid of those thoughts that say that you can't make it, or make you feel less of value! Wrong thought patterns keep us imprisoned in defeat.

- Break out of the limitations from the past and let the thoughts dwell around new, positive attitudes. Breaking these barriers will change your life!

Reveal those lies you might have believed in,- those that didn't bring you any further.

Establish new thought patterns;- did you know that it

only takes 30 days of conscious focus to establish a new habit?!

Maybe someone significant to you, has spoken negative words into your life. Maybe someone told you that you would never succeed, that you never will change or reach the top,- because you don't have what it takes to get there.

Don't listen to these lies!

No matter what you have been through in the past, no matter how many defeats you have experienced or who or what that has hindered your progressions,- it is a *new* day today!

Don't let your past decide your future!

Have you been treated unfair? Abandoned? Did anyone treat you bad?

Don't hold back the fantastic god-given future that lies in front of you, by dwelling in pain from the past.

For something new to appear in your life,- you have to do something new!

What you focus on will influence you. You will produce what you repeatedly visualize in your thoughts.

Are you feeding a picture of defeat and loss or of progress, hope and growth in your life?

Make room for growth in your own head. Visualize that you can reach your dreams.

Remember:

-this is a conscious choice that you choose to make. Or on the other hand,- you can choose to not make this choice. In both cases, these are choices *you* make,- but only the first choice will lead you forward. The second choice will keep you imprisoned in your existing thoughts and circumstances.

- You are the one in control. But you can choose to give it away.

-You can establish new thought patterns. Based on

what we have gone through until now, I believe that you now are convinced that this is possible.

A change demands perseverance and willingness to make some changes.

POWER-UP!

POWER-UP!

9. FROM DREAM TO REALITY

In this chapter the subjects that you have previous read about in this book will be transferred to questions. If you choose to use time to reflect on these questions, it will make you think about where you now stand; help you clarify your dreams and reveal negative patterns in your thoughts that hinder you to reach your dreams.

You should write down the answers, and be 100 % honest with yourself. Find a calm and quiet place, and answer one by one the questions. Take your time. Listen to your inside and to which type of thoughts that pops up in your consciousness. Look back and let your thoughts fly freely. Feel which thoughts that give you joy,- and the opposite; which thoughts are giving you dejection and negative feelings.

Questions to clarify your dreams

Most of these questions were also mentioned in chapter 2.

- What do you carry in your heart? What is your passion? What do you dream about doing or being?

- Is there something that you have a clear dream about doing or being, but for rational reasons have put away?

- What do you feel is your heart's deepest desire?

- Which thoughts, visions or dreams can you not get out of your mind?

- Where is your passion?

- What makes you enthusiastic even to talk about?

- Where do you produce good results?

- What feels natural for you to do?

- What type of assignments do you feel joy about doing?

- Are there any areas where your participation stimulate and "fire up" others?

- Which profession do you wish you had?

- If a miracle happened in your life, and there were no limitations for you to reach your goals,- what would it look like?

- If there were no limitations according to time, education or money,- where would you live, and what would you do for a living?

- Where do you wish you are in one year's time? What is your job? What do your surroundings look like?

Now that you know how negative thoughts are influencing your mind, your body and your future,- it is time for deciding to a) discover these minus-thoughts and b) replace them with new positive thoughts about yourself, your possibilities and your future.

Remember that *you* are the boss in your own life, and the saying "it is not how your surroundings are, but how you manage the surroundings" bears much truth.

You could have inherited negative thought patterns

from your family and your acquaintances. These patterns could have become your own, before you even knew that they didn't originate from you,- but just were thought patterns-, ways of behaving. Inherited when you were young (or older) from someone for you "significant other". That could for instance be from your mother, father, aunt, teacher, friend or others that have had influence in your life.

Decide today to work for breaking these negative thought- and behavioral patterns that continuously work at hindering you to achieve your goals.

Be nice to yourself, and help yourself to become a better version of yourself.

You *can* do it!

Questions to reveal limitations in your own thinking

Work with one question at a time. Dwell on them, let the thoughts come up from the sub-consciousness. Listen to how your inner voice is speaking to you throughout a whole day. Write the thoughts down and become aware of them. Keep a little notebook handy and write down your thoughts in different situations throughout one or a few days. I am sure that you will be surprised when you find out how you attribute and instruct yourself in certain circumstances.

Could it be that you are your own worst critic?

Could it be your own thoughts that is keeping you down?

Do you recognize thought patterns that you have heard before from your acquaintances or close family?

A person I know found out that she had a negative way of thinking about boyfriends. Based on some earlier negative experiences, she expected that men were egoistic and self-centered. Just by working on her own attitudes and expectations in this area, did she become aware of negative and destructive thought patterns towards men. That repeatedly led to negative expectations. And as we know,- negative expectations do not create positive experiences...

Only a zealous will-power, desire and perseverance to change this, will create results. A little step at a time.

I also want to give a little example from my own life. When I was 17-18 years old, I was an exchange student in Houston, Texas for a year. At that age, everyone took their driver's license test. I wanted very much to take my driver's license test while in the US, but my student exchange organization wouldn't permit it. When the year was finished, I went back to Norway, finished High School, and had a very kind boyfriend who drove me everywhere. At that time I had decided to become a professional model abroad and saved all my money for that. When I was 21 I carried out my dream about becoming a professional model, and lived three years in big cities like Milan, Hamburg, New York and Munich. In these cities it was common to travel by tram, so I never took my driver's license test.

A few years after I returned home to Norway, I started my studies in Oslo. Most students did not have a car, and neither did I. After these 7 years of studies were gone, I was 33 years old, and had now received an identity as a "non-driver". Not to drive had become so natural to me, that I didn't even reflect on it anymore. I was a "non-driver", and I had to arrange a lift with someone those times I did not take the bus. I managed well, and was mostly satisfied as a non-driver. I was "a person that didn't drive", and this was just how it was. I had subconsciously and also consciously, instilled myself that this is how things were.

In the mean time I had added that I wasn't a good driver either, and had really started to believe it. With the years passing by, I thought I was a person that didn't manage to learn how to drive a car. It was just the way things were, and I had accepted it.

Until one day. I had become 35 and overheard a comment from a family member of a person that was cognitive impaired,- who meant that this cognitive impaired person now should take his driver's license. When I heard that sentence, I pricked up my ears.

I started to reflect upon and evaluate my own situation. I thought and I thought and I searched for all possible reasons that could stop me in taking my driver's license. I actually did not find any!

I only found limiting thoughts in my own mind. That had given me an identity as "one who did not drive".

I started to work on my thoughts, and combined with the thought of not being able to pick up my own son in the evenings when he in some years would start being out late,- things changed. I decided to challenge myself. I ordered a place at a driving school, and after 5-6 weeks from I took my first driving class,- I got my driver's license!!

That was almost incredible to me. I did make it! On my first attempt also. And I had actually believed that I could not drive! I had even accepted it as a truth as well.

To me, this was a strong experience and support for the message in this book. If you don't dare to think new or take a first step, you can miss out on much in your own life!

I remember that I had made an inner picture of myself driving a car. I recalled this inner picture every day, and imagined how it was like to drive a car,- and how it was being "one who drives". This helped me creating a new identity as "one who drives a car".

This process actually demanded quite some effort from me. I have seen how this exact same process has been a piece of cake for my son, and many others. Maybe most others. They did not have that identity as a "non-driver" that I did,- and they have neither thought the thought that they could not, or would not, be able to take their driver's license. It has been the most normal thing to occur at the age of 18,- and from early on, most boys (and also many girls) have visualized themselves as drivers. That is an identity they have expected to occur.

I did not have such expectations.

That is why I had to work on getting them. This is the way we humans are created, and explains why we often end up in lives like our own parents, our surroundings and our friends. Upper class children grow up expecting to continue to live an upper class life. They put their expectations at that level. Limiting thought patterns and expectations can also be inherited.

Do you have some areas in your life where you have a

negative view of what you can *do*, *be* or *have*? Reflect on this and the questions that come in the next paragraph. This is important. If you receive clarity in such areas, it can lead you to go further in your own life.

- Which negative expectations have you settled with in your own life?

- What do you believe deep inside, are limiting you from reaching your goals?

- Do you believe that you are lord over your own circumstances? That you yourself are in charge of your life?

- Do you allow the Law of Jante (a Norwegian saying/"law" that says that you are of no worth and that you cannot achieve much) to stop you from doing, attempting or saying something to your own good?

- Are you repeatedly pulling up and reminding yourself of old negative occassions in your own life, or have you let them go and leaved them behind?

- Are you talking negative about yourself to others?

- Are you thinking negative thoughts about yourself and what you can achieve? What are these thoughts saying to you?

- Are you thinking negative thoughts that fill you with dissatisfaction, dejection, criticism or even hatred towards yourself?

- If you describe yourself with five words,- which words do you choose?

- If you have described yourself with negative words in the past question, ask yourself how long have these thought patterns been there. Decide to replace them with positive power thoughts about yourself.

- How much do you *really believe* you have the potential to achieve in your own personal life and in your working life?

- Which words do you think that your boss would use to describe you? Your spouse, a colleague, your childen?

If your answers to the questions above discovered that you have a negative view of yourself, a negative view of how far you can reach and if you believe that people refer to you negatively,- it is about time to replace these thoughts with positive plus-thoughts. Positive plus-thoughts about who you are and what you can do to become the best version of yourself.

Are you ready to go on?

If you have done the things that has been recommended so far in this book, you have now digged out your dreams and revealed hindrances and limitations in your thought life. You now also know that some of these potential negative thought patterns might have come from sources outside of you,- that were not even yours! No matter which source, you will now have to get rid of these negative minus-thoughts. They are like a backpack of negative ballast, that you must empty, in order to be able to walk with lighter steps into your future.

You now know that the instructions you give to yourself, and the glasses you see through, are of conclusive importance for how you think. In this, you can either further or limit yourself. You are the most important contributor to your own life.

Everyone may have been inflicted with negative influences from others, but we all have the possibility to raise ourselves up again. Have you heard about the "dandelion-children"? As a dandelion can grow in extremely hard surroundings; (have you seen it grow through asphalt?) – so can a child that grows up in bad surroundings also manage and become a beautiful flower. Be the one they were meant to be. Despite their surroundings and up-bringing.

It is of course harder. But it is not impossible. Everyone has, just as the dandelion that makes its way through the hindrances, the opportunity to force one's way through the negative and difficult growth- and environmental factors one could have been inflicted with. No matter the past, it can become a beautiful flower. We are created as to this being possible.

The belief in one's own ability to do it, will decide if one actually does.

If you do not have faith in yourself, you steal from yourself. You steal the joy to master new things and the joy to experience inspiring new happenings. Part of the joy of mastering, is to have dared to take a step out of one's own comfort-zone,- and to have mastered a challenge in one's own life.

If you are willing to take a few steps out of your own comfort zone,-much can happen. Yes, you expose yourself for failure, but the joy of mastering and winning over oneself is so incredible much larger than that! It is a much larger strain to go around being afraid of failure (and thereby not even making any attempts), than trying and knowing inside that you have done your best, no matter the outcome. Do you know that those people who have won much in life, have had to take steps into the unknown and have failed many times before they reached their goals? To fail is a part of being human, and for every time a person fails, the person becomes stronger and come closer to their goals. The person is one experience richer.

Most top athletes for instance, receive mental training. They daily practice visualizing themselves winning, and learn mechanisms to win over fear and fear of failing. They work on establishing good, cognitive thought patterns that give a positive profit in their lives.

So can you!

You CAN be a better version of yourself!

You CAN win over fear; fear of failure, fear of not being enough!

You CAN reach your goals and become a better version of yourself!

It gives a great joy to strive towards a goal. It also gives a great joy when one reaches a goal.

A very important part of it, is to recognize the negative thought patterns that stop you from going further in your own life. Mixed with belief in yourself and positive expectations. More about this in the next chapter.

POWER-UP!

10. BELIEF IN YOURSELF AND POSITIVE EXPECTATIONS

If you plan to become less that what you have opportunities to become, you will most likely be unhappy.

Abraham Maslow

To have faith in oneself is important, but to have positive expectations is of utmost importance. Chemers (1997) researched leaders and found that self- confidence was an important ingredient in making the leadership role effective, but the most important ingredient was a belief in one's own capacity to exercise the leadership role effective (Chemers, 1997). In other words, that means expectations towards own behavior.

Day, Hanson, Maltby, Proctor and Wood (2010) found in their research that the factor hope in a special and unique way could predict objective academic achievements above what intelligence, personality and earlier academic achievements did. These researchers found a significant positive similarity between students scoring high on the factor hope in their first year at the University and their later higher academic achievements (Day, Hanson, Maltby Proctor & Wood, 2010). The same results were found by Ciarrochi, Heaven and Davis (2007) who found in a study among 784 high-school students that hope predicted positive affect and was a strong indicator of the degrees. They also found that a negative attribution-style was the best predictor for increased fear, and that low self-confidence was the strongest predictor for an increase in sadness.

Throughout this book you have learned that by changing your way of looking at yourself and your expectations of who you are and what you can do,- can change your life.

Your own self-expectations is a strong steering factor in the process. By changing your thought patterns, you can change your life. You are the main producer over your own thoughts and you can yourself decide to work on your attitudes and thought patterns, so that you can become a better version of yourself. What you tell yourself that you can do and be,- will therefore influence on your future.

Now it is time to find your old list over limiting thought patterns that you have revealed through reading this book. You will now take one point at a time from this list, and replace the negative minus-thoughts with positive plus-thoughts. If you have revealed that you are feeding limiting thoughts like for instance "people like me do not manage to take a flight certificate" or "I do not have the intelligence for learning languages" or other limiting thoughts that you up to now have accepted as truth,- then now is the time to turn that particular thought process completely around. You shall now start to confess aloud to yourself that you can!

It can take some time to change a thought pattern, but one step must be the first step on the road. Let today

be the day that you take that first step. Dare to dream!
Dare to imagine. Visualize your dreams come true.

Make a list where you write down the opposite of those
limiting thoughts. Turn it around to a positive sentence
that says:

I can...

I can do.......….................….....................…................

I am...

Read these sentences aloud to yourself every day, and
visualize that you have reached your goals. Dwell daily
on these positive thoughts,- and decide to wave goodbye
to the destructive negative thoughts that you earlier
accepted into your thoughts. Stop saying limiting
statements about yourself. Arrest these thoughts and
limiting statements and decide to stop speaking
negatively about yourself to yourself and to others.
Change your vocabulary to speak about yourself and

your possibilities in a positive way. This will actually lead you to feel better. You have taken control over your own thoughts.

Becoming aware of your strong qualifications

To become aware of your strong qualifications, you will now continue to make a new list. This time the list should be threefold and have the following headings:

1) My positive traits and characteristics:

....

....

....

....

....

....

2) What I am good at:

....

....

....

....

....

....

3) Positive comments and feedback I have received:

....

....

....

....

....

....

This list is important for making oneself conscious of one's already existing strong traits and characteristics. Everyone is not always aware of their positive characteristics. If this is the case for you, then a talk with a good friend, one whom you trust,- would be helpful for giving you some honest feedback.

POWER-UP!

POWER-UP!

11. LONG-TERM AND SHORT-TERM GOALS

The value of having clear goals are of conclusive importance. To hit the bull's eye requires that you have focused on the target. To be goal-focused means that you have made some goals and that you are focusing on them. You need to be goal oriented to reach the goals that you already have, or shortly will make.

In this book these goals will be based on what you have discovered about yourself so far; your dreams and the hindrances that you have revealed in your thoughts that are in the way for you reaching your goals.

Fortunately you have received many confirmations to why you have been thinking the way you have in certain settings, but also according to what you can instill in yourself to reach in the future. Just as driving a car, the eyes must focus far in front, and not only on the steering wheel or on the car right in front of you.

You will experience that when you have made your goals clear, you have already come a long way. You know where to put your energy,- and in which direction to drive. Would you travel in a boat without a compass? It would be like driving without knowing in which direction you are going. Your goals for your life work as a compass that gives your life direction.

In the next section you will write down your own goals, based on what you have clarified so far.

Long-term goals

Write down the date today, a date in half a year, one year or maybe two-three years. Maybe even longer.

-Where do you want to go? How will you achieve it?

- How are you going to achieve it?

- What do you need to achieve it?

Visualize it. See what you have accomplished. What does it look like when you have reached your goals? Where are you in life?

Where do you work and what is your profession? Which new skill sets have you learned? Note what it looks like when you have reached this big goal.

Hide the picture of success in your inner, and take it out every day. Let it be alive for you on your inside. You should preferably only work towards one big goal at a time.

It is best to focus 100% on one goal at a time. When you have reached one big goal, you can make new ones. Write down the goal, the date and a concrete description of how you know that the goal is attained. Your table can for instance something like this:

Date today:	Goals and sub-goals:	Date when the goals have been reached:	How will I reach the goal?	What do I need to reach the goal?	How do I know that the goal has been reached? Hallmarks.

Table 3. Goals

Short-term goals

Most likely do your long-term goal(s) consists of many short-term goals. You must divide your long-term goals into smaller short-term goals that need to be reached. Thereafter you must set a date to when they will be reached. Maybe you need to learn some English because you want to have a job with much traveling? Maybe you need a boat certificate to get a job in the marine sector? Maybe you need to start saving money so that you can afford a car that you need to be able to do other things?

What if you have behavioral goals; like for instance controlling your temper. In that case, a short-term goal could be to start controlling oneself by counting to ten in given situations. Another short-term goal could be to start to search for and focus on positive aspects in the person you're mad at. These are just a few examples of short-term goals. You must find yours, and write them down. Like in the section for goals above, also in this section the short-term goals must be described concretely with dates, how you know when you have reached the goal and so on.

- When you have clarified your goals, you will also feel the motivation to fulfill-

POWER-UP!

12. THE IMPORTANCE OF DISIPLINE, FOCUS AND PERSEVERANCE

To know is not enough, we must implement. To wish is not enough, we must do.

Johann von Goethe

Now that you have gone through the processes of clarifying your dreams, revealed hindrances in your own thoughts, attitudes, and made concrete goals, there are a few extra things you need to take into consideration. Discipline is important. Discipline is what drives you forward and is an important ingredient when you attempt to achieve your goals!

If you are a person that has fed your own thoughts to

believe that you are not disciplined enough, and that you cannot reach your goals,- you must take some steps back and let this be a concrete goal to work towards. You must also work on replacing these thoughts with thoughts that tell you that you can reach your goals! You must start feeding yourself with positive thoughts about yourself being able to discipline yourself. You can,- just as much as others can. If X can do it, surely can you.

Going back to my story about taking the driver's license test, it was exactly the thought that if a person that had a lighter cognitive impairment could manage to take the driver's license (those around him believed he could), that released a new set of thoughts in me. If he, with such large difficulties could manage,- could I also?! There and then my thought pattern changed from "impossible" to "maybe possible". The rest of the story you have read in an earlier chapter.

An expectation turns into an attitude, and an attitude turns into a thought. Repetitions of these thoughts can become a habit.

If you decide to be nice to yourself, you do all that

you can to show some discipline in establishing new thought patterns. If it takes 30 days to establish a new pattern, that is 30 days of bigger challenges, before you have established another level of thinking.

It is of course also important that you keep your focus on your goals and what needs to be done to achieve these goals. You must discipline yourself to dwell on new positive thoughts and on your possibilities. You must also continuously focus on the long-term and short-term goals. This is of utmost importance for you on your way to become a better version of yourself! Read your plan daily. Be zealous and exhibit perseverance.

If you continue this establishing of new thought patterns, it is guaranteed that you will be satisfied with yourself in some time! Give yourself a chance to be good to yourself! You are the one who wins the most by challenging yourself to establish new positive habits.

Additionally, in social environments there will be a more positive and enthusiastic version of you. Enthusiasm is catching, and people like to be around positive people. The new attitudes will radiate out of you. People will show you more respect, and if you remember what was written in the chapter about expectations from others, you understand that this is creating a new positive spiral in your life.

The fact that other people have positive expectations of you, will again lead to you having a more positive picture of,- and more positive expectations to yourself. These expectations will lead you to position yourself at a higher level of mastering than what you otherwise would have done. This is a win-win situation.

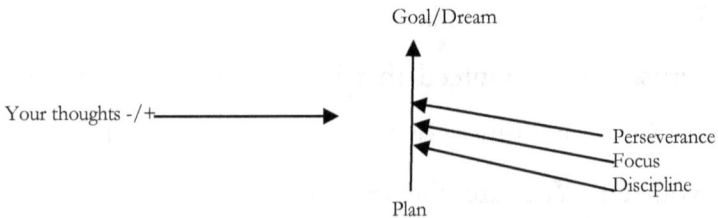

Figure 2. Important elements in goal-setting. Your plus- or minus-thoughts, your perseverance, focus and your discipline are influencing your plan of reaching your goals and dreams.

We are what we repeatedly times do. Excellence is therefore not an attitude, but a habit.

Aristotle

POWER-UP!

13. YOU CAN!

So what are you waiting for?

There is no longer any doubt that YOU can! That you can be a player in your own life and master over your own thoughts.

YOU can uncover limitations in your thoughts that have hindered you to become a better version of yourself,- and YOU can replace them with new and positive thoughts about yourself.

You have now learned that your expectations towards yourself influence on how far you can go. When you take some grips and replace those "liar-thoughts" about yourself with positive thoughts about who you are and what you can achieve,- then change will actually happen.

This is no hocus pocus, but a long-term planned change of old and negative thought patterns.

Remember it is never too late to start! No matter how many times you previously failed, all of these times have actually contributed to making you stronger. You can take some grips on your own life, and decide to work with yourself. There are no quick ways, and it demands that you:

1) Decide to take charge over your own future- and desire to become a better version of yourself.

2) Thereafter searching out your dreams and

3) Clarify which limitations within yourself are hindering you to achieve your goals. Your goals must be concrete, measurable and time given.

4) With the ingredients of discipline, focus and perseverance, you have the rest of what you need.

So what are you waiting for? Take the first steps towards becoming a better version of YOU!

Remember that:

"You are never given a dream, without the ability to fulfill it"

and that:

For something new to appear in your life you have to do something new!

Go for it!

POWER-UP!

ABOUT THE AUTHOR

Merethe is currently a third year Ph.D.-student in Organizational Leadership at School of Business and Leadership, Regent University, Viriginia Beach, USA.
She has worked 8 years as a personnel manager and five years as a pedagogical-psychological advisor. She has been a speaker and in charge of many conferences in the field of leadership, motivation and development.

Merethe is passionate about people and development, both at work and in her spare time. She loves to help people to discover and use their potential and to become the best versions of themselves!

POWER-UP!

REFERENCES

Balthazard, P, Waldman, D.A., Rhatcher, R.W. & Hannag, S.T. (2011). Diffferentiating transformational and non-transformational leadership on the basis of neurological imaging. *The Leadership Quarterly* 23, 244-258. doi:10.1016/j.leaqua.2011.08.002.

Bandura, A. (1977). Self-efficacy: Toward a unifying theory of behavioral change. *Psychological Review* 84, 237-239.

Bannink, F. P. (2006). The Birth of Solution-Focused Cognitive Behavior Therapy. *Behavior Therapy* 39(3), 171–183.

Bannink, F. P. (2005). The Power of Solution-Focused Therapy: A Form of Behavior Therapy. *Behaviour Therapy* 38 (1), 5-16.

Bannink, F. P. (2006). Solution-Focused Mediation. *Journal of Conflict Resolution* 7, 143–145.

Bannink, F. P. (2007). Solution-Focused Brief Therapy. *Journal of Contemporary Psychotherapy* 37(2), 87–94.

Baumeister, Roy F., et al. (2012). Control deprivation and styles of thinking. *Journal of Personality and Social*

Psychology 102 (3), 460-468. http://0-dx.doi.org.library.regent.edu/10.1037/a0026316

Bar-Tal, D. & Frieze, I. (1976). Attribution of success and failure for actors and observers. *Journal of Research in Personality* 10, 256-265.

Bar-Tal, D. & Frieze, I. (1977). Achievement motivation of males and females as a determinant of attributions for success and failure. *Sex Roles* 3, 301-313.

Bauer, J.J. & Bonanno, G.A. (2001). I can, I Do, I Am: The narrative differentiation of self-efficacy and other self-evaluations while adapting to bereavement. *Journal of research in Personality* 35, 424-448.

Bronfenbrenner, U., & Morris, P.A. (1998). *The Ecology of Developmental processes.* In: W.

Demon (Series Ed.) & R.M. Lemer (VoI.Ed.), *Handbook of Child Psychology*: Vol.1 Theory (5th Ed.). New York: Wiley.

Bronfenbrenner, U. (1995). Developmental Ecology Through Space and Time: A Future Perspective. In Moen, P. Elder, G.H. and Luscher, K. (Eds.), *Examining lives in context: Perspectives on the ecology of human development.* Washington, D.C: APA Books.

Cauffman, L. (2003). *Solution-Focused Management and*

Coaching. Utrecht: Lemma.

Chemers, M.M., Watson, C.B. and May, S.T. (2000). Dispositional affect and leadership effectiveness: a comparison of self-esteem, optimism, and efficacy. *Personality and Social Psychology Bulletin* 26(3), 267-277.

Ciarrochi, J., Heaven, P.C.L. and Davies, F. (2007). The impact of hope, self-esteem and attributional style on adolescents' school grades and emotional well-being. A longitudinal study. *Journal of Research in Personality* 47, 1161-1178. doi:10.1016/j.jrp.2007.02.001.

Day, L., Hanson, K., Maltby, J Proctor, c & wood, A. (2010). Hope uniquely predicts objective academic achievement above intelligence, personality and previous academic achievement. *Journal of Research in Personality* 44, 550-553. doi:10.1016/j.jrp.2010.05.009

Deaux, K. (1976). Sex: A perspective on the attribution process. In J. H. Harvey, W. Ickes & R. Ki dd (Eds), *New Directions in Attribution Research, vol. 1.* Hillsdale, NJ: Erlbaum.

Decker, K.S. (2008). The Evolution of the psychical element George Herbert Mead at the University of Chicago Lecture notes by H. Heath Bawden 1899-1900. *Transactions of the Charles S. Peirce Society* 44 (3), 469-479.

De Shazer, S. (1985). *Keys to Solution in Brief Therapy.* New York: Norton.

De Shazer, S. (1994). *Words Were Originally Magic.* New York: Norton.

Farwell, L., and Weiner, B. (1996). Self-perception of fairness in individual and group contexts. *Personal Social Psychol. Bull.* 22, 867–881.

Goei, S. L., and Bannink, F. P. (2005). Solution-Focused Remedial Teaching. *Dutch Journal of Learning and Behavior Problems* 5(3), 19–26.

Gottschall & Stefanou. (2011).The effects of on-going consultation for accomodating students with disabilities on teachers self-eficacy and learned helplessness. *Education* 132 (2), 321-331.

Guest, D., Peccei, R & Rosenthal, P. (1996). Gender differences in manager's causal explanations for their work performance: a study in two organizations. *Journal of Occupational and Organizational Psychology* 69 (2), 145-157.

Green, P. (2008). This is your brain on happiness. *The Oprah Magazine*, March, 230-235.

Kidd, R. (Eds), *New Directions in Attribution Research,* vol. 1. Hillsdale, NJ: Erlbaum.

Kirsch, I., Deacon, B. & Huedo-Medina, T. (2008).

Initial severity and antidepressant benefits; a meta-analysis of data submitted to the Food and Drug Administration. *PLOS Medicine* 5 (2), 260-268.

Imsen, G. (1991). *Elevens verden.* Oslo: Tano.

Lebedina-Manzoni, M. (2004). To what students attribute their academic success and unsuccess. *Education* 124 (4), 699-708.

Leuchter, A., Cook, I., Witte, E. & Morgan (2002). Changes in brain function of depressed subjects during treatment with placebo. *American journal of Psychiatry* 206, 122-129.

Martin, J. (2005). Perspectival Selves in Interaction with Others: Re-reading G.H. Mead's Social Psychology. *Journal for the Theory of Social Behaviour* 35 (3), 231-252.

Martin, j. & Gillespie, A. (2010). A neo-Meadian approach to human agency: relating the social and the psychological in the ontogenesis of perspective-coordinating persons. *Integrative Psychological and Behavioral Science* 44 (3), 252- 268.

Paglis, L.L. (2010). Leadership self-efficacy: research findings and practical applications. *Journal of Management Development* 29 (9), 771-782.

Paus, T., Petrides, M., Evans, A. C., & Meyer, E.

(1993). Role of human anterior cingulate cortex in the control of oculomotor, manual and speech responses: A positron emission tomography study. *Journal of Neurophysiology* 70, 453–469.

Pryce, C.R., Azzinnari, D. Spinelli, S., Seifritz, E., Tegethof, M. & Meinlschmidt, G. (2011). Helplessness: A systematic translational review of theory and evidence for its relevance to understanding and treating depression. *Pharmacology & Therapeutics* 132 (3), 242–267.

Rock, D. & Schwartz, J. (2007). The Neuroscience of Leadership. *Brain and Behavior* 16(3), 10-17.

Rosenthal, R. & Jacobsen, L. (1977). *Pygmalion i klasseværelset.* København, Danmark.

Rosenthal, R. (1979). *Conceiving the self.* New York: New York.

Ruddick, F. (2008). Hope, optimism and expextations. *Mental health practice* 12 (1), 33-35.

Seligman, M. & Csikszentmihalyi, M. (2000). Positive psychology: an introduction. *American Psychologist* 55 (1), 5-14.

Stams, G. J., Dekovic, M., Buist, K., and de Vries, L. (2006). Efficacy of Solution-Focused Brief Therapy: A Meta-Analysis. *Behavior Therapy* 39(2), 81–94.

Tissinton, L.D. (2008). A Bronfenbrenner Ecological Perspective on the Transition to Teaching for Alternative Certification. *Journal of Instructional Psychology* 35 (1), 106-1110.

Walker, C.M. (2010). George Herbert Mead: an overview and understanding of symbolic interactionism. *The Proceedings of the Laurel Highlands Communications Conference* (annual 2010), 221- 233.

Weinberg, R.S., Hughes, H.H., Critelli, J.W., England, R. & Jackson, A. (1984). Effects of preexisting and manipulated self-efficacy on weight loss in a self-control program. *Journal of Research in Personality* 18(3), 352-358.

Weiner, B. (1979). A theory of motivation for some classroom experiences. *Journal of Educational Psychology* 71, 2-25. Weiner, B. (1986). An Attributional Theory of Motivation and Emotion, New York: Springer Verlag.

Weiner, B. (1992). *Human Motivation: Metaphors, Theories, and Research.* Newbury Park, CA: Sage.

Weiner, B. (1995). *Judgement of Responsibility: A Foundation for A Theory of Social Conduct,* New York: Guilford.

Weiner, B., Graham, S., and Reyna, C. (1997). An attributional examination of retributive versus utilitarian philosophies of punishment. *Social Justice Res.* 10: 431-452.

Weiner, B. & Kukla, A. (1970). An attributional analysis of achievement motivation. **Social Psychology** 15, 1–20.

Weiner, B. (2000). Intrapersonal and Interpersonal Theories of Motivation from an Attributional Perspective. *Educational Psychology Review* 12 (1), 1-14.

Whiteley, P., Sy, T. and Johnson, S.K. (2012). Leaders' conceptions of followers: Implications for naturally occurring Pygmalion effects. *The Leadership Quarterly* 23, 822-834. philosophies of punishment. *Social Justice Res.* 10: 431- 452.

Weiner, B. & Kukla, A. (1970). An attributional analysis of achievement motivation. *Social Psychology* 15, 1–20.

Weiner, B. (2000). Intrapersonal and Interpersonal Theories of Motivation from an Attributional Perspective. *Educational Psychology Review* 12 (1), 1-14.

Whiteley, P., Sy, T. and Johnson, S.K. (2012). Leaders' conceptions of followers: Implications for naturally occurring Pygmalion effects. *The Leadership Quarterly* 23, 822-834.

www.ingramcontent.com/pod-product-compliance
Lightning Source LLC
Chambersburg PA
CBHW061747270326
41928CB00011B/2410